Not My Grandmother's Hymnal

Composing a Curious Faith

Rebecca Wilson

Copyright © 2025 by Rebecca Wilson

All rights reserved.

No part of this book may be reproduced in any form or by any electronic or mechanical means, including information storage and retrieval systems, without written permission from the author, except for the use of brief quotations in a book review.

Tehom Center Publishing is a 501(c)3 nonprofit publishing feminist and queer authors, with a commitment to elevate BIPOC writers.

Paperback ISBN: 978-1-966655-70-1

Ebook ISBN: 978-1-966655-71-8

Contents

Acknowledgments   9
Introduction   11

Gospel Truths

Take Me To Church   17
Good   21
There's More   22
Born Again   25
New Laces   26
All In   30
Eleven   31
Not My Grandmother's Hymnal   35
Graveyards   36
Linwood Trees   38
Or Shall We   41
Wrapped   43
Too Much   45
Raptures and Hurricanes   47
Bones Alive   52

Deep Listening

Footsteps   57
Storm Tracking   59
Extinguish   62
Detention   63
Cry Room   67
Hour of Deportation   69
Easy Peace   74
Prayer of Roe   76
Keep Silent   79
Do We Hear It   80
Erased   83
Poured Out   85
White Smoke   87

Holy Days

Ascension	93
Aha	96
Burned	98
Afraid	100
Longest Night	102
No Vacancy	104
Virgin Births	107
Super Glue	109
Tradition Tells Me	111
Breaking In	112
Clowning Around	116
Unleavened	119
Our Feet	121
Patent Pending	125
Smirk	127

Sacramental Supplements

Homesick	131
Quality over Quantity	135
Healing	136
Smile	139
Lois	140
Head in the Clouds	144
Inquire Within	145
Quarters	149
For the Day You Baptize a Book	150
Daily Bread	153
Fragile Things	154
Appetite Change	155

Synchronizing

All Seems Lost	161
Truth Be Told	165
Hold On	166
Things I Can Trust Right Now	169
Left Wondering	172
That's When	174
Learning to Walk in the Dark	175
Asked to Define Success	179

Card for Coming Out	180
Ready or Not	183
Small Print	188
Requirements	189
Invitation	193

To Grandma Bernie for the faith you gifted me. The only photograph I have of us together is fuzzy, yet your impact on my life is as clear as an up north summer morning sky over Lake Huron.

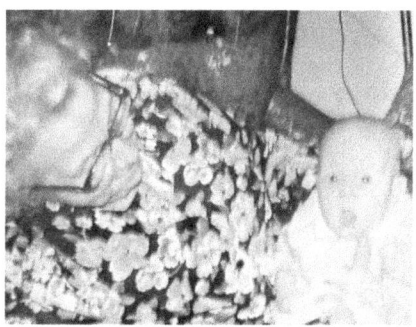

To all the grandmothers who have loved and nurtured me, inspired and ignited my curiosity.

To everyone who opens this hymnal, may you find your song.

Acknowledgments

Shortly before signing a contract with Tehom Center Publishing for *Unraveling: Coming Out and Back Together*, I shared an idea of launching a poetry show, *New Laces in Old Shoes*, with a friend. Six poems interspersed with personal stories meant to challenge, inspire, and entertain. Much to my delight and surprise, the show took off. Taking on a life of its own as a supplement to *Unraveling*.

From Michigan to Florida, to Maryland and Delaware, to Oregon and back home, I shared my heart and voice with curious audiences. Discovering to be true what I always suspected, poetry is a form of storytelling and telling stories is a sacrament of healing. Healing for the one who tells and the one who listens to the story. Poetry speaks truths in ways that other modes of communicating cannot. Poetry opens lines of connection that other forms of conversation do not. Poetry builds community that other materials will not.

The initial outline of my second book of poetry was shaped around the poems of *New Laces in Old Shoes*. But the more I worked on that manuscript, the less confident I became in where it was leading. I knew those poems were part of the project, but would they define it? I told myself to keep on writing and revising, and trusting that the details would come to light.

And they did. Brightly. Boldly. Brilliantly. Beautifully. *Not My Grandmother's Hymnal* came to me as I walked toward Haystack Rock in Cannon Beach, Oregon. Sitting on a long piece of driftwood —with a copy of *Unraveling* in one hand and a souvenir copy of the treasure map from *The Goonies* in the other—what you have in your hands now was born.

Suddenly the vision was clear. A bunch of pieces, piles of pages, pain and promises, revealed the next chapter of an exciting ever-unfolding journey. A journey made possible by the many individuals who have and continue to believe in me, especially when I've struggled to believe in myself and the transformational work of 10CAMELS.

Deep gratitude to family, friends, subscribers, and followers who read my words and also listen to my wild ideas and extravagant dreams.

Sincere appreciation to the churches and groups that hosted poetry shows and book events. And to the person who stayed to the very end to share, "I didn't think I liked poetry, but you've made me a believer."

A special word of thanks to Rev. Dr. Angela Yarber, founder and Executive Director of Tehom Center Publishing, for her commitment to elevating feminist, queer, and BIPOC voices and for the community of revolutionary authors she has built and nourishes.

Introduction

There is a church nearby. Though I have never worshipped there, its music occupies a space within me. The hymns coming from the bell tower everyday are forever embossed on my heart.

Most days, like today, when I take a morning walk with my dog, without effort or intention, I find myself singing along. A few notes is all it takes to name the tune. I also hear the hymns from inside the house, usually before anyone else. I'm not listening for them, but they find me. Remind me of a faith I used to hold. Many nights, like tonight, as the setting sun sets the sky ablaze with vibrant shades of orange and red, I am humming along to a tune taught to me by my great-grandmother.

Growing up I had four grandmothers; a maternal and paternal grandmother and two great-grandmothers on my mother's side. While each of them in uniquely distinct ways has shaped who I am and what I believe, one of my great-grandmothers had a particularly profound impact on my faith.

Grandma Bernie, as I affectionately called her, was a devout Methodist. Rooted in the teachings of John and Charles Wesley as much as she was in Jesus. Where there was a bible, there was a hymnal too. Both treated as sacred texts.

Our connection was special and unexplainable, and not without tension. As her oldest great-grandchild I knew her in ways others did not. I associated her with images found in the hymnal she gifted me, that still rests on my desk. A lighthouse, a rock in a weary land, a lily in the valley, a strong foundation in a house of sinking sand.

She was strongly opinionated and prone to voicing her convictions, including that girls should wear dresses, slips, and tights; that attending church on Sunday was a requirement not a choice; that alcohol, like cussing, was sinful.

A year before she died, I spent the summer with her and my great-grandfather at their cottage in northern Michigan on the shores of Lake Huron. That time together, allowed me to experience another side of her and for us to get to know each other in a deeper way. She was nearing 90 years old, her health declining, her spirit wrestling, her heart grieving for a family and world she struggled to recognize. Through stories of her life from childhood forward, I learned more of what she believed and how she came to believe it. Born in the first decade of the 1900s, she had seen life I'd only ever read about. In a society where she knew very few rights and privileges beyond being a wife and mother, church was a place where she held positions of influence and power, where lifelong bonds of friendships and mutual support were formed.

One morning that summer, I woke to discover a large pimple on my face. Grandma Bernie saw it right away. When I started to cry she asked what the tears were for. I told her I was ashamed because I didn't know how to take care of my skin, that no one had ever taught me what products to use and how to use them. She told me to bring her pocketbook from the bedroom. She opened it slowly and handed me two ten-dollar bills. Then proceeded to gently instruct me on what cleanser and moisturizer to buy from the drugstore in town. And with a wink she said "keep the change."

At the core Grandma Bernie's faith was a call to love god, neighbor, and self. As I've become less focused on how to "rightly" love god, my ability to fully love myself has strengthened. My desire and commitment to love my neighbor has intensified. My courage to speak against judgement and injustice disguised as love continues to grow.

At the age of 18, around the time of Grandma Bernie's death, propelled by worsening depression, I began wandering from the United Methodist Church toward Pentecostalism. In the bigger picture, my time there was short and spread out over many years, but the toll it took reaches far into the marrow of my spirit. Strangely it was the faith of my birth that pulled me from that fundamentalist fire pit, cared for my wounds, brought me to a place of healing, nurtured and endorsed my call to ministry. Only to then say, I had to choose between being queer and being ordained.

It is easy to hear the morning hymns from the bell tower and feel rising sadness and anger. Remembering how the church I loved was not a safe harbor, but rather the cause of a storm I nearly didn't survive. It is not difficult to hear the evening hymns and feel comfort and connection. Remembering the ways church was a balm before it became a poison.

There are days when I wish I could erase all the hymn tunes and lyrics from my memory and my bones. Yet, for better and for worse they are part of me. So, what do I do with them? I allow them to guide me. Not toward a denomination, physical church building, or strict doctrines of belief, but rather toward an inquisitive searching faith.

Not My Grandmother's Hymnal is a continuation of my story. A story that is more curious than certain. What does it sound like to leave church and still wonder about god? To name your trauma as a path to healing from it? To remember the past without sacrificing the future? To celebrate your own light? To examine the words you sing and what they really mean? To refuse to continue singing about theology you no longer believe? To step away from the faith of your grandmother and compose a faith of your own?

We cannot unlearn what we know, but we can change what we do with the knowledge we hold. We cannot simply forget the people and places that shaped us, but we can create new patterns of formation. We cannot silence the bell tower, but we can choose where the music leads.

I often wonder what Grandma Bernie would think about me today. How would she respond to my queerness and my unraveling? I don't know for sure, but remembering the ways she showed me how to care for my skin, I imagine something soft and similar for my spirit.

These poems, like hymns, reflect a variety of styles and rhythms, topics and themes, experiences and perspectives. The choruses and refrains may feel familiar or untouchable. Individually, they may stir healing or bring memories of harm to the surface; affirm your doubts or challenge your beliefs. Collectively, may they be softness for your spirit and water for the curious faith you are creatively composing.

Gospel Truths

in event of rapture or hurricane I'll be right here

Take Me To Church

take me to church
to a brick house
with a peace
      pole
in the front yard
just the other side
of the city line

to a home where a six-year-old
serves as director of hospitality
taking coats with a full smile
sharing about a half day off from school

to a living room
with children's art on the walls
ink marks on the chairs

to the edge of a wobbly coffee table
filled with wine, water, cheese, sausage
where there's a plate
waiting to hold
chocolate chip cookies baking in the oven

   take me to church
to a space where faces reflect diversity
of race, culture, experience
where eyes are free to cry
tears are met with support
weeping is contagious

to a group where hands can raise
when honest testimonies
fill our hearts with praise

where pastors driving Porsches
passing parishioners
at the bus stop
are ridiculed
where exploitation of the poor
is loudly condemned
humiliation of the vulnerable
is damned and not amen-ed

   take me to church
to the moment where authenticity
is encouraged
conformity is discouraged
the discouraged are encouraged
to acknowledge the impossibility
of perfection

   take me to church
to the realization that church
is where god is
the reminder that god is everywhere
god is always and forever love
everyone is with god
woe to those who preach a message
contrary to this one

   take me to church
to a community of sinners and saints
where bricks and mortar
ain't the real foundation
where it all rests on relationship
the strong and weak link up tall together
so nobody
          falls

   take me to church
where poetry and prophecy

are hard to distinguish
where words have power to light fires
a world of injustice cannot extinguish

   take me to church
where the flame drives us
warms, inspires, convicts us
is never ever the thing that burns us

   take me to church
pull me in
nudge me in
dancing, singing
invite me in
to the prayers and the dreaming

   take me to church
where giving
opens the door to receiving
all meals are holy and filling
every recipe has eternal meaning

   take me to church
where my whole self
is welcomed and loved
my demons are exercised
not judged
my scars are celebrated as victory
not diagnosed as insanity

where healing flows
new hopes grow
miracles happen
eggs scramble in the toaster
answers are less important
   than questions

where drag queens call us
from the　　　　　margin
proudly to the
　　　center
preaching the gospel
through good ole bingo numbers

　take me to church
like the one
I imagine we build together
where there are no buildings
　　or christians
just creation believing in each other

Good

not always the best word
but such a common one
    morning, day
    afternoon, evening
    night, bye
    luck, riddance
    grief, going

in the eye of the beholder
like beauty, but sharper
subjective and perspective
we say it without thinking
without pausing
to consider its meaning

like this news
    confusing, conflicting
    depressing, uplifting
like an earthquake
    a shifting
a lightning storm
    a quickening
a power outage
    a reckoning

when the light returns
will we re-examine
    dying, living
what we mean when we say

good

There's More

someone said
if you put a seashell up to your ear
you can hear the shore
I was so excited
then I realized you could hear the same sound
from a shoe or a cup
or anything else you put up to your ear

you do not need a shell
to hear the shore
or a magnifying glass to know there's more

I'm a little embarrassed to admit this
I used to memorize bible verses for badges
I was a Pioneer Girl
like a Girl Scout without cookies
we traded thin mints
for a taste of good christian living
the first verse I ever memorized
Matthew 5:14 & 15, King James Version
I sounded something like this

> *ye are the light of the world*
> *a city that is set on a hill cannot be hidden*
> *neither do men light a candle*
> *and put it under a bushel,*
> *but on a candlestick*
> *and it giveth light unto all that are in the house*

the scripture I knew it
got the fuzzy badge to prove it
never imagined there was more to it

more than memorizing lines in red
regurgitating what someone else says
more to belief than believing
in the resurrection of the dead

I did more than memorize
I rapped, beat boxed and all
in the fellowship hall
at the Lady's Spring Tea
everyone in flowered dresses
fancy hats and me
in an orange t-shirt
green and purple strangely patterned
petal pushers
the 80's version of capris

I rapped facing the wall
not the crowd
even then I knew there was more

they didn't respect me
they pitied me
put me in the program to convert
not to uplift me
to lift up the false notion
they appreciated diversity
to teach me
the only way I could be anything
was to be what they determined worthy

next time you will wear a flowered dress

that performance left me a mess
I received a candle for my service
it was never ever lit

that city on a hill that cannot be hidden
that lamp shining for all to see
what if it's us

   what if
we are more
more than genetics
and geographic location
our parents' occupation
our gender and sexual orientation
the church's evaluation

   what if
we are less the problem
more the solution

   what if
we refuse to use a lack of sea shells
and magnifying glasses as excuse

   what if
we believe in the resurrection
of the living

   what if
we remind them there's more
another verse
not required memorization
more than important than the first

Matthew 5.16, it goes like this

let *your* light shine!
there's more of *you* this world needs to see

Born Again

neighbors saying
my faith meant nothing
if I hadn't been saved
praying the sinner's prayer
born again

again at church camp
emotions stoked
around a hot fire
counselors testifying of past sins
running to a splintered altar

and again right around the time
I was praying daily to die
a pastor laying hands
telling me unless born again
I'd never see god's kingdom
only strengthening my belief
I was better off dead

that was decades ago
I've been living ever since
even before I knew
being born again
   not by blood or shame
     but by love and faith
   not by fear or scorn
     but by water I am born
again and again

New Laces

I almost failed kindergarten
because I couldn't tie my shoes
   fact or fiction?
I'll leave that up to you

lied to my dad
told him if we had Velcro
we didn't have to take the test
the rest of the story

I had to tie my teacher's orthopedics
made no bow only a knot
while she cut it out
I went to the naughty spot
   one might say
here began my fascination
with sneakers and shoe laces

second grade I learned
shoes are the soul of being cool
overjoyed for a pair of all white
high top
   Prokicks
     from Picway
with interchangeable multi-colored laces

before the laces started fraying
or the rubber started fading
a classmate broke it down for me

and I took a
   tumble
      down
the playground social
la--dd--er
fancy laces do not matter
when you're still wearing generics

second grade was a fall
but third grade was a cliMB
for the first time
sporting brand name shoes

orange, white and blue Patrick Ewing Adidas
everything I dreamed of and more
my cool factor soared
no longer the white girl
picked last for kickball
now playing with the big ballers
aiming for the rusty metal rim
with no net in the parking lot

fourth grade, I hit the jackpot
a pair of gray snake skin Lottos

fifth grade, I was tight
Hammer Pants, pink and white British Knights

sixth grade…

seventh grade
sweetest bluest Nikes you'd ever seen
living the dream

eighth grade
not one but two pair of shoes
Rebooks and K-Swiss

ninth grade
fine in some fly green Filas
ah, you can't touch this

shoes were more than shoes
where I existed
my classmates and I
all given the same message
you're good for nothing
we had to have something
to give us pride and playground position
we discovered quickly
the key to survival
could be found in a shoe

Vacation Bible School Jesus said
no one puts new wine in old skins
that wouldn't have made sense
where I was living
only attention given to wine
was when the party store changed the sign
   Boones Farm: 3 for $5

now if Jesus said
no one puts new laces in old shoes
that might have pulled me in

back to grade six
the year there were no new shoes
no good news
the year even a pair of Air Jordans
couldn't have improved

bad decisions and health conditions
left my family in disarray
soles and souls were shredded
we'd never be the same

my aunt took me to the thrift store
in exchange for babysitting
bought me a 50¢ pair of kicks
no name, no logo, no laces
black high-tops with a torn tongue
and Velcro at the ankle that didn't stick

with a marker I covered up the scratches
with scraped up coins
bought some matching laces
even though I knew
and everybody knew
those shoes were used
weaving in new laces kept my spirit alive
kept me going when the madness of home
left me wanting to die

sixth grade is forever with me
memories didn't kill me
but haven't left me
even barefoot walk beside me

>   I am who I am because I was who I was
>   because I saw evil I'm committed to love

it's less about skins and wines
shoes and laces
more about what we do
in the face of unspeakable tragedy
realizing yet not settling
for an unjust reality

had Jesus said
I make all sneakers shiny and new
I would have gotten saved much sooner

All In

I was all in
hook
line
sinker

when I was sinking
they didn't care
about the good fishing I'd done
only that who I was
was against the rules
they selectively broke
and sanctimoniously followed

we prayed as I drowned
sunk before they said
amen

Eleven

11
the first time I saw someone die
my dad and I
visited an old guy in the hospital
on the way to watch basketball

he was 95
battling pneumonia
at the foot of his bed
the nurse said
that gurgling sound he's making
he's taking his last breath

just like that
he was dead
Jesus
remember him when he comes into your kingdom

15
the second time
my grandma
who hadn't really been alive for years

she was 55
fighting to survive
though the tubes had long been unplugged
I knew now
that gurgling sound she was making
she was taking her last breath

before I could forgive
she was dead

Jesus
remember her when she comes into your kingdom

18
when all those memories
gripped me so tightly
I believed the only option was letting go
I didn't know
another way

someone…help me…please…

can't sleep
I wake to the sound of troubled breathing
can't live the weight of their dying
so heavy on my heart
there's no space—there—for—beating

Jesus
remember me if I come into your kingdom

he had been juror and judge
waiting to punish me because
I was selfish, weak
foolish enough to think I could take a drink
a drag and not get hooked

god a distant father
resembling the failure of my own
nothing I could ever do
would ever earn his love

church a source of blame
faith another reason for shame
fought like hell
harvesting mustard seeds

to be told repeatedly
it wasn't enough

I can't pin point when
wasn't a moment
but a collection of them
wasn't a day or a night
but a series of them
leading to a familiar rugged cross
a passion play
with props covered in blood
where I was told to make a choice

looked up
there he was
with criminals, suspects, outcasts
dirty, naked, exposed, rejected
like I had been
embarrassed, ashamed
angry, betrayed
like I had been

one acting out
one apologetic
one hurling insults
arrogant, proud
one a little more repentant
seeking Jesus' favor
not the crowds'

I saw myself in both of them
how tragedy drew me to this lord
but also left me hating him
I saw myself in both of them
calling on his name
but also cursing him

Jesus, one said
remember me when you come into your kingdom

I still remember
the choice
letting myself be crucified
in hopes of finding paradise

once I was 11 years old

Not My Grandmother's Hymnal

they haunt me, guide me
ghosts or angels
depending on the time of day
piano, organ, acapella
on water drops in the shower

I know the lyrics, the tunes
stories behind them
meaning inside them
theology hiding within them

I'm like a jukebox of old songs
feed me a quarter
I'll play your favorite
pick a scripture to go with it
my heart is filled with her favorites
Amazing Grace
In the Garden
Great is Thy Faithfulness
Love Divine All Love Excelling
my whole being is swelling
with grief, all the losses
her and the church she gave me
the beliefs they taught me
my mind is swirling
with curiosity, possibility

invite me in, I'll tell you a story
composing a faith not found
in my grandmother's hymnal

Graveyards

I learned it at church camp
holding your breath
when you ride past a cemetery
so you don't breathe in
spirits of the dead

the camp was on the bay
but we couldn't swim on that shore
twice during the week
they loaded us on buses
drove us to a nearby beach
known for its sandbars
so shallow, yet so deep

we sang catchy choruses
with dangerous messages
about heaven and hell
who goes where
except for when we stopped
to hold our breath
watching graveyards go by
like moving trains
passing side by side
the motion made me nauseous
   I hear they put in a pool
     and-----a zip line

superstitions
I still believe some of them
part of me still remembers
how they told us around hot camp fires
right before bed
when we were still cold from the lake

that we'd burn forever
if we didn't accept Jesus now

nothing can enter a heart
that has taught itself
how not to breathe
as a way to survive

yet, in those breathless moments
I hear a voice as clear as breath
calling me to share life with those
who've been scared to death
by people with no idea
what it means to be alive
because they've been breathing in
deadly spirits every summer
of their whole lives
on holy campgrounds
that closely resemble graveyards

where songs, arts and crafts, games
even the snacks are weapons

where water
isn't suitable for swimming

where fruity punch
they call communion
is ripe for drinking

where childhood
like god goes to die

Linwood Trees

life has taught me
death comes with autumn
falling leaves and closing caskets
weathered baskets
filled with wilting flowers
long days
nights of bedside visits
cold rains, strong winds
a strange stirring in my spirit

faith teaches me
resurrection is reserved for spring
rolling stones and empty graves
mourning prayers turned to praise
linens gone
bodies raised
mysterious gardeners
angels say
why do you seek the living among the dead

these lessons pull at me
like I pulled on the string
of the hooded knit cardigan
I wore as a child
it didn't fit
it never fit
one sleeve longer than the other
zipper never zipped
but I couldn't let go of it

these lessons remind me
if I'm open life will continue surprising me

seasons change
so do emotions inside of me

right on time
autumn has arrived
the chill in the air
cloudy skies rolling in
just like memories
of the nightmares I lived

but today in the most amazing way
it feels like spring
less like October
more like May

the heaviness on my chest
isn't the pressure of death
the terror of frantically gasping for breath
it's hope nursing at my breast
rising like a robin from its nest
singing to the world
anticipating what's next

I'm pulling at the pockets on my jacket
I guess a nervous habit
as I do
that childhood cardigan begins to unravel
the grandmother's hands that made it
start to fade
patterns she left on my body
get harder to trace
her grave no longer calling my name
I speak of her
with less fear and shame
no longer content to wear clothes
carry guilts that do not fit
I wonder what has changed

after some walking
the answer rides in on a breeze
that gently stirs the Linwood trees

I'm not alone
let others in
learned to trust
to ask for help and support
found the courage
to uncover the wounds
express my doubts
dare to share my hopes and dreams

like seeking out
my great-great uncle Alex's grave
saying aloud
why I'm so drawn to his name

laughing, smiling
imagining his dapper designs
handsome jaw line
reflecting on the ways his living
is similar to mine

if following Jesus teaches anything

    resurrection isn't tied to a season

Or Shall We

we shall not be moved
or shall we?

moving about I've come to believe
we can move and be still simultaneously
stillness moves us unexpectedly

trees that shall not be moved
are not entirely still
they are filled with courage and strength
bend, might even br--e--ak
regrow miraculously
acknowledging the pain they feel
   and the harm they've caused

generations unending
roots eternally spreading
understanding the oxygen
   released helps others breathe
knowing they need
you and **me** to be healthy
   for **we** to succeed
recognizing they began with a seed
   that someone else nourished and watered
sharing their berries without conditions
   shade has no borders

when the church tells some
we don't belong
their branches turning to home
     leaves fading into pews
   wind becoming song
       trunks ringing good news

I worship there
when no one else will have me

reminding, creation begins in a garden
inviting us over to play and pray
sit and get comfy, messy in the dirt
muddy in the soil, bearing fruit
resting after toil
not resisting transition
immersing ourselves in sacredness
mysteries surrounding us
cherishing the journey, wherever it leads
cultivating delight

oh, the ways we might be surprised
when we see with our hearts
love with our eyes
move not only our feet
but also our minds
envisioning sanctuaries
      as extensions of eden
blooming with glory
scripture as river, flowing with story

I chose a path I didn't want to take
and that has made all the difference
  away from everything
  I'd ever known
closer to who I was born
to god's heartbeat and our own

singing
yes, we shall all be moved

Wrapped

   a preacher I once knew used to say
let's be Jesus with skin on
this always made me itch

I've tried to redeem the image
almost as much as I've worked
to redeem my body and my spirit
from the harm inflicted
by this preacher's condemnation
   of queerness

while my redemption is well underway
and I'm stronger
more whole everyday
the call to be Jesus with skin on
still is a scratch

until today
when I heard another say
if Paul's similes
metaphors or images
don't work for you
imagine ones that do

I don't want to put Jesus' skin on
I want to love my own
speak hope and healing to those told
that for their flesh and being
   for whatever reason one can list
   they are undeserving of god's abiding love

I want to wrap myself
in all that Jesus lived

died teaching us
compassion, peace, grace, mercy
equality, equity, justice, jubilee

not like a mummy is wrapped in bandages
but the way one wraps a warm quilt
around a friend preparing for their last breath

a freshly washed blanket
over a rescue dog scared by a hurricane

a handmade scarf
around the neck of a child shivering
from the cold water they just escaped
now separated from their parents at the border

a hug
around a mother whose son
has been shot in another act of violence

foil around a hot sandwich
for a neighbor who hasn't eaten in days

I want to be wrapped
in everything Jesus modeled

leave his dead skin alone

Too Much

take a deep breath in
   a sip of water
   a bite
of something sweet or salty
or both or neither
take a break
from whatever sits before you
the endless cycle of news
debates
decisions
of wars
and weather systems

take a walk
   a closer look
   at what's before you
your dog
flowers
freshly cut grass
your neighbors playing pickleball
kids learning to ride bikes
without training wheels
a strange pile of shoes
near a picnic table
take a guess
how they got there
take a piece of paper
   pen
write a story about them

take a moment
minute
hour

morning
afternoon
evening
an all day nap
a respite
refresher
a really hot
or super cold shower
take whatever you need
to not surrender to the pressure

take in the little reminders
   that life is possible
   even when powers that be
viciously and violently
remind us how close
we are to danger

exhale
as a protest
life preserver
energy source
and compassion conserver

take up space
take all your steps
take hold of the hopes
                        that linger
they are key
to our survival

Raptures and Hurricanes

I sometimes wish
I believed in the rapture
that god, like a hurricane
would come in and *whirl* us away
save us from the problems we've created
pick up the mess
we've made of ourselves and creation
    but, god is love
    and love doesn't work that way

in event of rapture this car will be unmanned

a bumper sticker on a van
in the church parking lot
I asked one of the elders
    what if there's other people in the car

looking back I wonder
how I got caught up with a group of people
whose entire faith is based on a god
who takes it all away
whose response to every ill
pain, problem, sin
is to pray it all away

depressed, lost, lonely
only eighteen
desperately needing direction
attention
walking a -----tight rope-----
toward self-destruction
when a co-worker invited me to church

a slow introduction
carefully skilled induction
it all came to a head
an exPLOSion
during a Sunday night revival

that morning the preacher
railed against sinful items and behaviors
cigarettes, alcohol, drugs, sex, masturbation
medication for depression
secular music and films
anything Disney, and of course, homosexuality
the holy ghost told him to tell us
bring it all to the fire, pray it away
I sort of believed him

so I filled my backpack
with a pack of Marlboros, vodka
marijuana, a vibrator, Prozac, Tupac CDs
VHS copies of my favorite movies
The Incredibly True Adventure of Two Girls in Love
The Little Mermaid

the moment it all went into the fire
I held my b-r-e-a-t-h
my knees l-o-c-k-e-d
as booze stoked the flames
weed permeated the air
I almost passed out from fear

as a chorus of *hallelujah*
thank you Jesus rang out
as more fuel was added to the fire
folks began to wildly shout
I knew I was in over my head

praying for god to come down
and pull me out
whirl me away like a hurricane

a week later
smoking more than ever
drinking earlier and longer
listening to rap music on the radio
dreaming about adventure with the girl I loved
feeling like a failure, a freak
believing there were demons
roaming inside of me
needing to be prayed away

to the same elders overseeing the fire
I didn't say no when they came
to lay hands on me
one PRESSED my forehead
like he was pressing a cantaloupe
to see if it was ripe
another pushed so hard on my skull
I felt my brain move

they just kept screaming
louder and angrier
in a language that sounded like
Spanish and Star Trek
I fell back
it was the only way I knew to escape
slaying myself in the spirit
to be raptured away
I didn't know any other way
to save myself
there are no hurricanes in Michigan

a church mother
covered me in a sheet

stood over me
praying it all away

what she didn't know
because I could not say
depression, drugs, self-destruction
suicidal ideation
all because I hated myself
for being gay
and hated god for not hearing my prayers
to take it away

I saw the arsonist on YouTube
telling his new flock about that night
how lives were changed
strongholds burned, depravity swept away
still ranting against homosexuals
now vaccines, masks
liberals, democrats
wanting to make america great again
begging Jesus to come back
redeem this evil nation

I'm reminded rapture
isn't the only way to get free
from tribulation
grateful for the ones who saved me
from that congregation
brought me to a new salvation
who said, you are perfect and loved
just as you are and were created

but I sometimes still wish
I could believe in the rapture
that god
like a hurricane
would come *whirl* us away

it would be easier that way
than believing in a god
coming to us
in burning bushes on mountaintops
hazy backpacks
in pentecostally paved parking lots
inspiring us to do the work of healing
making meaning of the wilderness
wrestling with our calling
what it means to be beloved

decades later
still sifting through the ashes
picking up the pieces
piecing myself back together
queerer than ever
proud to say I smell like smoke
because I survived unholy fire

in event of rapture or hurricane
I'll be right here

sharing hope and love
with others the church left behind

put that on a bumper sticker

Bones Alive

yes, these bones
broken bones
still not fully healed
dry, cracked, fragile bones
can live

here is how I know

I've had broken fingers
wrists, arms
ankles, collar bones
I've worn splints
braces, plaster casts
hopped on crutches
lay on the sidewalk with a bone
protruding from my body
a hole in my chin needing stitches
a rusty green bike
with busted handlebars and a bent rim
blocks from the house
wondering how I'd make it home

I've had my spirit crushed
dreams and dignity shattered
been cut
    off
from one family
when I told the truth about violence

gently
    shunned
by another

when I realized the closet
was no longer habitable

like skeleton pieces
set out on a lab table
in the biology class I failed
I examine my life

how despite the pain
trauma, wounds and scars
I'm living
prophesying over myself
asking the same spirit
that inspired visions
   wheels in the sky
   chariots on high
   dead bones coming to life
enliven me to be
one whose being
shows the world
dead things can live again

every time it rains
through the pain of brokenness
I remember
I'm alive

hope is not gone
these bones
my bones
your bones
   living
   moving
   breathing
   seeking
     our way home

Deep Listening

make a garden call it a cry room

Footsteps

prayer sounds like
    footsteps
one in front of the other

made with a rhythmic combination
of hope and trepidation
travel to a place I've never been
with people I've not yet met
to study a language
experience a culture not my own

to learn liberation
perhaps to find purpose
meaning again
or to breathe joy
grace again

as I move the prayers do too
goosebumps on my heart
    gratitude
for health, endurance, perseverance
shivering down my spine
realization

as I fly comfortably by choice
others below are
    floating
evacuated from flood ravaged homes
streets still inundated with rain
pain in my gut
reminder

as I freely visit a country
some are
      fleeing
with relative ease
    passing through checkpoints
that leave them detained
conviction

plastic bound pages in my hand
a passport
privilege sounds like
   footsteps

Storm Tracking

a hurricane is coming this way
still waiting on a name
the most up to date landfall location

it's been a slow season
the disaster kit
I keep in the closet running low
I go to fill it
already toilet paper
paper towel aisles empty
canned food gone
I get Pop-Tarts
peanut butter, bread
the last 12 pack of water
what is it about storms and viruses
that turns us into hoarders

I have a conversation with a guy
who believes by tracking the storm
I'm living in fear rather than faith

he says
god won't let the storm hit here
because he knows
we have a lot of old people in town

I ask
what about the old people
and all the people in other towns
god is okay with them in harm's way

he insists
I'm not going to argue with you

I have faith, just have faith
that god won't let the storm hit here

I think
oh sir, that's not faith
that's the kind of faith to fear

the storm has a name now
Ian

I go to the beach before it closes
to talk to a god with many names

asking that everyone be prepared and protected
that the poor, the vulnerable
those already inundated
with the stress of harsh living conditions
swaying in the winds of seasonal depression
will not bear the brunt of this tropical destruction

that there will be enough food
clean water to go around
lost things all get found
in the wake of heavy waves
dreams and homes, lives won't drown

that we will pray less, do more
come to realize our actions feed these storms
our choices and consumption
turn up the temperature of air and ocean
how our arrogance and indifference
the ballots we cast
escalate rapid acceleration

that we would never again
turn our eyes
because they track away from us

toward our neighbor

that we wouldn't wish for
another location to be a hurricane destination
that we might be spared

that we lay to rest once and for all
a god who sends storms as punishment
cast-off religion that equates
being in the eye of a hurricane
as being removed from god's grace

that local meteorologists wouldn't get excited
when the storm turns west
it's not a competition
there is life there too
another's pain is not our good news
every spaghetti model leads to suffering

no power in days, no phone signal
elevator out
I walk a few steps down the stairs
water everywhere
my dog needs to pee
alligators in the streets

who's tracking this?

Extinguish

it's when I am the saddest
that I grieve the fiercest
   for the church
not the building
but the community
the people that taught me
home and family
   love is a verb

only to turn belonging
   and calling
into a weapon
   formed against me
while the world around us burns
I'm frightened
   with nowhere to go

and so I go
   where light
has always been
never fails to welcome me

returning to the land
to walk the path
   that heals me
listening for how my hands
worn and tired
   as they may be

bring water
   rather than gas
to the fire

Detention

everything that happened that day
makes me question

what is liberty? who's in captivity?
is justice for all or just for some?

we came seeking entrance
to a center of detention
the government calls it
   a dormitory
they came seeking futures
in this country of dreams
a system calls them illegal

our IDs taken
matched up with applications
all in the name of safety
their jump suits and wristbands
not orange but green
numbers more than names
all to maintain order

together at a table
ten minutes of conversation
hardly enough time for disclaimers

I'm not an attorney
I cannot give advice
I'm here to show that someone cares
I need to verify your A Number

the four of us
two in green

two in disbelief joined hands
prayed that god grant us
   strength and patience
to their families
   peace and assurance

one guard pointed them
   back to their cells
another told me to leave

your driver's license doesn't match
you're unauthorized to be here
there's nothing else I can tell you

afraid
embarrassed
what did my colleagues
assume about this
isolated, anxious
I sat in the lobby
on a cheap foam seat
looking around

pay phone, water fountain, pop machine
television with a note saying
do not touch
another warning visitors
all conversation is monitored and recorded
an electronic cashier
no sign saying *welcome*
exit sign most will never encounter
two deputies watching me
from behind the glassed-in counter
with two hours to wait
plenty of time to wonder

feeling helpless
   trapped
   between
   four make shift walls

not the experience I volunteered for
motive was pure
done nothing wrong
but feel so guilty
watched, judged
I just wanted
to do something good
make a difference

my mind wandered
   behind locked doors
what was going on back there

feeling helpless, detained
separated
from everyone   everything I know

trapped in a
10 x 6 cell
not the journey I expected
intention was simple
now branded a criminal
guilty by birth
no chance of a trial
every move surveyed
just wanted a chance at life

everything that happened that day
fear, frustration
I lived through that day
do not compare
to the cold reality alive in there

in the end welcomed in
two months later
misplaced paperwork
a mishandled application
it had all been a mistake

in the end the two men in green
were loaded on a bus one night
driven an hour in the dark
put on a flight
that may or may not
have taken them home

everything that happened that day
causes me to question

who's profiting from detention?

Cry Room

at the church
where I was raised
babies stayed in a nursery
in a building
separate
from the sanctuary

when I went to catholic mass
with my other grandparents
I was fascinated
by the cry room in the back
with sound proof glass

god forbid
lord have mercy
if a cry or fuss
were heard
in worship

seen
not heard
   mandated presence
   mum is the word
you are welcome
you don't belong
   pain and joy
   must be stifled
shame the mothers
   who like Mary
   only as holy
as their oldest son

they teach us
   not to cry
in public
   no politics
in the pulpit

praise god at all times
   especially the hard ones
no questions or doubts

beating into us
that bad times
are the best times
to let gratitude ring out
loud enough to drown
dis
   tract
      ions
like a newborn baby
cooing or calling for milk

building a church today?
   forget the walls
   and glass
   plant trees
   seed the grass
   make a garden
  call it a cry room
where tears
water
revolution

Hour of Deportation

Santa Maria
  Madre de Dios
    llena eres de gracia

I met Jesús
it went much like I expected
his american dream melted
when ICE arrested him
after a traffic stop
he asked
could I get word to his mother
that he was okay
I said I'd try
scribbled a number on a scrap of paper
nervously called several times later
ring, ring, ring

no one ever answered
I thought about Mary in a garden
calling out to a son
who couldn't answer

then I met Muhammad
just a few years younger than me
inquisitive, skeptical like me

why was I there
he wondered
was it really ok for us to speak
what do christians really believe

our every move observed
every whisper overheard

by guards
the same ones who removed me
the first time
I came to visit immigrants
imprisoned in the county jail
it was an error on their part
although they'd never admit it
they did let me back in

there I was again
face to face
with Muhammad
fielding questions
about sin and salvation
how much I knew about Islam

he knew more about Mother Mary
than my catholic grandmother
who hails her every morning
told me all the passages in the Quran about her
then he told me about his own mother
how he's a disappointment to her
how he fell in with a bad crowd
trying to support his sister
an unwed pregnant teenage mother
how that falling
came back to haunt him
right before his MBA program was over
leading to his arrest

did I know that Prophet Muhammad
peace be upon him
lost his mother when he was just a child
I thought about Jesus
sleeping in a manger
a cold and musty stable
so holy, so meek, so mild

Jesus came to set the captives free
they arrested him and sentenced him to death
one empire crucified his body
we watch in crowds
as another mutilates his message

Jesús came to the United States
as a baby
swaddled in the arms of his mother
across a human made
violently conquered border
following a star
lit with the hope of something better
brighter
now scheduled for deportation
back to country he's never known
a language he doesn't speak
his crime
running a stop sign

Muhammad said with determination
I'm not fighting deportation
just waiting for a flight
hoping my wife will forgive me
for destroying both our lives
that there's still a chance
to make my mother proud

he asked
what does the bible say
about forgiveness
can god forgive me

before I could answer
he continued telling me
all the things he's done wrong
mistakes he's made

prayers he hasn't prayed
drugs he sold to ensure bills were paid

he took a breath
just long enough for me to ask
can you forgive yourself

and then like soldiers to the cross
the guards came to our side
time was up
the visit over
Muhammad leaned
over
   the table
said
bless you

I thought about Jesús
Jesus and Mary
what it means to carry
heavy burdens
empire puts upon our backs
shoulders
how they bury us
grieve our mothers
teach us to imprison strangers
telling us
it's a way
to love our neighbors
that sin is in our hearts
not the systems that arrest us

that grace—like green cards
passports and visas—is restricted
that for as low
as 5 million dollars you can get it
throw in extra to have it

overnight expedited
packaged in gold

by powers—that deny Christ entry
raid hospitals, schools,
sanctuaries—we are told
freedom is uniquely christian
I could never have more in common
with Muhammad than with Jesus
I'm a disappointment too
to the mother who birthed me

I'm not worthy
I still haven't suffered enough
for God to forgive me
self-forgiveness means nothing

Santa María
  Madre de Dios
    as-salamu alaykum
pray for us now
in this hour of deportation

Easy Peace

  it's easy
to pray for peace
when missiles are launched
rockets fly
when drones take off
bombs
     drop
when buildings
col—lap—s—e
sirens ring out

  it's harder
when skies are quiet
the subjugated and oppressed
are silently moving about
navigating embargoes
checkpoints
ruins and rubble of home

when history is hidden
re-written to protect power
when news is narrated
in the voice of the powerful
when we've bought into the fantasy
that every situation has
two sides
   good
  and
   bad
people
living on both

there's more than two sides
two kinds of people
there's no winner in violent games
the less one has when it starts
the more they lose when it's over

is it ever really over
again and again
we discover

this type of fighting
is so profitable
for those who already have
so much
so devastating for those who survive on
so little

   it's easy
to pray for peace
when creation is covered in smoke

   it's harder
when the horizon is clear

   it's easy
to pray for peace

   it's hard
getting harder
to imagine
this world
without
war

Prayer of Roe

mystery, beyond our imagination
close enough for us to gather
   under your wings
embrace us in this moment of
breathlessness, sadness, grief
fear, shock and anger

some of us are stunned
others expected the outcome
our collective emotions are
   c O n T r A c T i N g
by the announcement
for some the words are many
for others silence is our response

yes, o living one
life is precious and beautiful
so too is freedom and self-determination

yes, o holy one
birth and birthing is holy
so too is choice and personal decision
access to care, infertility
in vitro, contraception
miscarriage, postpartum depression

yes, o sacred one
babies are sacred and blessed
so too are toddlers and teenagers
adults, elders
those who don't believe in Jesus
   or religion
other paths to you

yes, o creator
creation is marvelous
so is sex for procreation and pleasure
doctors who perform abortions
regardless of trimester
those who choose to have one
for any and all reasons
they choose to have one

clinics who offer pap smears
birth control, mammograms
hormones, therapy

marvelous too are black lives
trans bodies
queer relationships

grace us space
to regain our breath
hold us long enough
to capture our sadness
comfort our grief, still our fears
ease our shock
acknowledge our lack of surprise

then baptize our anger
that within us
new resolve might arise
and too be called beloved
that might we organize
to stop this backwards march
this power grab
this attempted coup
of uterus and womb
this white supremacist army taunting us
in broad sunlight
under the breached banner of

c h r I S T I A N i t y
quoting prophets they'd turn away
from the communion table
plotting their next repeal

for our safety
our dignity, rights, privacy
our coming together
the humanity and health of all
we pray in the sweet, wild
revolutionary name of Mary
who bore and carried the divine
that we might have choice
in whether or not to do the same

some intersessions
cannot end with
amen

Keep Silent

I'll keep silent
before I post a platitude
   or a beatitude
about who is blessed right now

I'll keep silent
before I quote a scripture
   or a hymn from a religion
that is complicit
in getting us where we are right now

I'll restrain from rushing
from hushing others' pain
from speaking into the void
while denying the hole
in my whole being
the way whiteness
      centers
        my
       spirit

I'll keep silent
while I try to be still
knowing nothing
except
I am
unsure
of everything

Do We Hear It

fired from one side
   a declaration of war
from another
   a response to terror

my nation's bombs a defense
   yours a crime against humanity
both weapons of destruction

strategic, miscalculated
warning, last resort
targeted, unprovoked
all deadly
generations in the making

innocent bloodshed or
evil to be destroyed
who decides?
the same voices
enticing us to choose
their side

protecting borders
or imploding them
like guns drawn
with full knowledge of their power
this level of violence is catastrophic
unsustainable
we've lost count of bodies
so many souls

judging selectively
assessing differently

justifying swiftly
condemning ruthlessly
celebrating callously
revenging heinously
repeating shamelessly
accepting effortlessly
over   over   over
    and   and

as talking heads debate
which casualties are necessary
demand annihilation
best further our own cause
some receive aid
others cut off
   even further
     from humanity
       and provisions

more and more people die
more and more wounded
suffer and hide

more and more of creation burns
more and more hearts
turn to a cold state
believing this is simply unavoidable fate
another reason to hate our neighbor
obliterate our enemy

might we cry for all the children
every child orphaned
scarred
killed by war
abandoned by a world
deeming their living
and their lives expendable

above the bunkers
below the rockets
a siren song
composed of mothering cries
playing in the background
of our grandfathers' wars
every continent
ocean
faith has a chorus
knows the haunting refrain

do we hear it?
our collective heartache
our universal hope
like peace is fragile
risky
needing constant tending
listen deeply
prayerfully
curiously
let it be louder than resignation
let it be an awakening
a call to ending these unwinnable wars

do we hear it?

place your palm upon your chest
maybe we are meant to feel it

Erased

cropped out
of a family photo

my name
~~taken off a list~~
of past clergy recipients
of a justice award
after I
    surrendered
my credentials
the work I'd done
no
  longer
      mattered

this is what I feel
remember
reading
the T and Q
were
~~removed~~
from the Stonewall National Monument

there is no Stonewall
without trans and queer people
of color
no rainbow
without black and brown

erasure and deletion
painful and hard to
      s-w-a-l-
          l-o-w

doesn't actually do
what it says
I'm still here
we're still here
shining magical brilliant letters
without us
all your words are

incomplete

Poured Out

high upon the wall
between two gothic windows
hangs a bronzed bible
and a large rimmed chalice

what if it spills, I thought
what if the blood
some 2,000 years fermenting
spilled out once and for all
every last drop
drip
    ping
on the marble floor
wooden pews
stone columns
left to dry
like bones after the body dies
flesh decomposes

never again served
to unsuspecting guests
as sips of poison
judgement
damnation
dressed up as mercy
forgiveness
reward

never again
weaponized
withheld from thirsty spirits
parched lips

what if it spills, I wondered
right after it's filled with water
from the fountain in the square
or from the river down the hill

what if that ancient water
was poured out on everyone
without exceptions
exclusions
no prerequisites or conditions
continually, forever, always, eternally
on all the people

heads, hands, feet
eyes, lips
hearts, souls, spirits
hopes, dreams, sorrows, griefs
a cleansing, a healing
a filling, an in-filling
of love, grace, goodness

what if everyone who drinks
from the cup
then takes a pitcher
full of living water
everyone served serves another

suddenly the words
written on ageless pages
  hanging on a wall
  in a bronzed book
unopened for centuries
come alive

White Smoke

a statue in
my grandparents' garden
perfectly placed
   among flowers
   and stones
tended to with great care
devotion
it wasn't Jesus
but a saint
resembling him

Peter, Paul, John
Benedict, Francis
   I don't remember
it definitely wasn't Mary
she was in the bedroom
near the kneeler
for morning rosary

they taught me about cardinals
the seeds
   attracting them
   to the feeder
how to identify them
the brilliant red reserved for males

my grandpa
   artist, skeptic, man of a million words
   I inherited his curiosity and questions
made me feel less like an outcast
as a methodist kid
in a mass full of catholics

his silence
   after I came out to him
   in the shadows
   as he watered azaleas
   and she pulled weeds
    be happy he didn't say anything bad
still gives me pause

like the one
dressed in fresh linens
folding into the light
on the heels of white smoke

as people preach
   their peace
quickly embracing
his chosen name
   Leo
downplaying the doubts
and hopes
of those historically
   devoured
by lions
who refuse to romanticize
the separation of sheep and goats
the union of empire and eden
to bless the middle
   road
where the margins
get hit head on

you're right
I don't have a stake
or place
or vote
in this or any church
anymore

but that doesn't
~~void~~ my wonder

maybe we'll be surprised
at who is allowed
   to drink from the fountain
maybe we'll listen
   to the songs of birds
eating at different tables

Holy Days

how we live our lives when the flame goes out

Ascension

I remember taking a kite to the playground
on a pretty still day
with little wind
struggling to get it into the air
I was 10
and convinced myself
that if I could get a kite high enough
to touch a cloud
I could
pull
a piece
back

    d
      o
         w
            n

to earth
and hold it
it would feel like cotton candy

I'd been told
heaven was in the clouds
god was there
Jesus and angels
all the faithful people I'd known
who died

I'd recently read the book of Revelation
becoming terrified of hell

fire
demons
certain I wasn't good enough
to spend eternity
in the good place
with streets of gold
and crystal stairs

that piece of cloud
was my only chance
of getting close to god

the wind picked up
the string snapped
and the kite was carried away

I spent the afternoon
walking the neighborhood
searching
in gated backyards
I never found it

finally
I've quit looking up
in search of god
or some heaven in the sky
holy is right here
mystery alive right now
in our hands
beneath our feet
like cotton candy
sticking to our fingers
melting to our teeth
perspective changed
when my faith

d
e
d
n
e
c
s
a

Aha

what if Pentecost
isn't a birthday celebration
but an ongoing Epiphany occasion
a dramatic **aha** moment

that the church isn't ours
the earth isn't ours
it belongs to creation

that we are called to love
ourselves
in the same measure as
god and neighbor
that fire is a source
of life **and** destruction
requiring both care **and** caution

that our language isn't superior
the Spirit speaks through tongues
of those we outcast
and label stranger
that the miracle of a million voices
isn't who is speaking
but who will dare to listen
how we navigate the silence
interpret the translation

that the real power of the anointing
is how we live our lives
when the flame
goes
   out
the music

    f   ade   s
the prayers
   -cease-
the sermon
ends.

signs and wonders
give way to
the ordinary

Burned

just a kid the first time
I remember
being burned by church
so excited
finally old enough to acolyte

a little too eager to bring in the light
touching the tip of my finger
on the flame
ashamed
not wanting anyone to know
suffered in silence
secretly blowing
wrapping it tightly
in the sleeve of my robe
pressure helping ease the pain

seeing the baptismal font
from where I sat
wanting so bad to dip the
t
 i
  p
of my finger
in the cool water to stop the sting

not the last time I was burned by church
kept the pain to myself
sitting anxiously
in a sanctuary
longing for healing water

as the church celebrates this Pentecost
recalling calling down fire
praying for power
I pray for me
for you
for all who've been burned by church
whose finger tips
and hearts are marked
by flames of judgement
rejection, cruelty, hatred
disguised as good news
justified as adherence to tradition and rules

for everyone who's sat
in a hard hot pew
longing for water reserved for a few
I'm sorry you've been burned too
I'm angry the church is baking birthday cake
when what we ache for
is a cup of ice water

I'm wading in the river

>   *let anyone who is thirsty come*
>   *let all who wonder drink*
>   *come as you're ready*
>   *we will drink together*
>   *may you feel these drops of water*
>   *poured out for you*
>   *may they be soothing as they bead*
>   *on the tips of your fingers*
>   *may they bubble love on your lips*
>   *and taste like healing*
>   *on the way to your heart*

Afraid

I am afraid
as sickness and disease surround me
a mask covers my face
which I know is a form of protection
  but in this moment
  feels like it's choking me

monitors are flashing brightly
beeping loudly
people screaming
  moaning, coding

one in handcuffs
demanding more juice and crackers
another on a cell phone cussing
because the Subway order
didn't come with a cookie
a young pregnant woman
doubled over in pain
someone asking
  if I've seen their brother
  they cannot find him

my mother like so many others
floating in a hallway full of gurneys
when I finally find her
I lay my coat over her
because she's freezing
blankets like rooms are scarce
  we both are weeping and afraid

I am plagued by ancient tapes
recorded by old preachers

evangelists, grifters, traveling healers
well-meaning people
equating fear with unforgivable sin
   lack of faith
   even insanity
a sure way to displease god
and betray Jesus
land yourself in an eternal lake of fire

here I sit
except for when I'm standing
to get out of the way
at the end of her bed
in a wooden folding chair
pushed against the nurses' station
   waiting, watching
afraid and doubly afraid of my fear
feeling weak for not being stronger
for my inability to command this feeling
   to flee

praying to a god
I'm not so sure I really still believe in
   please don't come here
or send some messenger
to tell me not to be afraid
because I am
because behold I'm holding
an unbearable load of fear

what I really long to hear is
   it's okay to be afraid
   I am fearful with you

Longest Night

I wish someone had told me sooner
some nights are longer than others

some cuts burn deeper
some pains run sharper
some hurts traveler further
that sometimes loneliness
and grief can alter
the rhythms
----
of your heart
sweeping you
off
   your
      feet
like an unexpected dance partner

it wasn't all in my head

some nights
really are longer
tonight really is
the longest of the year

that's me
you'll see twirling
   under
   the
   stars
cold breeze pulling me in
chilly air pushing me out
I'll find my rhythm
even though I've never

found the beat

deeply breathing
as the solstice is stirring
   I think
   I might
be healing

my heart
spirit
mind
being
all s t r e t c h i n g
toward the realization
longest isn't synonymous
   with hardest
night doesn't always rhyme
   with sorrow
moon is often brighter than sun

if only we allow ourselves
to bend
   bow
   believe
in that direction

because no one told me sooner
I'm sharing with you now
may this guide you
   through
this longest night
we are waltzing
   through
right now

No Vacancy

we say
we are awaiting his return
that we must be ready
at all times

he will come
   in the twinkling of an eye
riding on a cloud
shining like the sun
if we are not careful, attentive
we will miss him

miss out on eternity
in paradise
   left behind
   left to ward off
demons, devastation
ultimately burn in hell
face unending damnation

well, he came
none of us were ready
we did not simply blink
we missed him completely
   knowingly, willingly
closed our eyes

he was riding on a tire
crafted into a raft
never meant to float
the open seas

his family risked their lives
not for paradise, but survival
leaving behind ancestral home
no longer able to hold
militants at bay
options for food
   exhausted
water…run…dry
staying a sure death
leaving a long shot
the only way left to try

professing to love a savior
only able to offer salvation
because when the inn keeper
refused to open the door
his parents had the audacity
to turn a barn
   into a birthing stable

how can we ignore the
   knocking
cheering for inn keepers
frantically posting
   no vacancy signs
in every window

claiming to follow a savior
only able to save us
because when his family
was forced to flee their home
they found refuge in another land

how can we go on about our day
leave them prey
to the same enemies
we claim threaten us

looking for his return
we missed his coming
   patrolling gates
   policing borders
   othering neighbors
we denied him entrance

Sunday we will cry out
  Jesus come quickly

if we stopped singing
our hymns so loudly
we would hear
him crying

  I was a refugee
    you turned me
      away

Virgin Births

she was a young maiden
depending on translation
maybe 11
her description
    pregnant yet also a virgin

I have an aversion to this word
phantom screams
from this same age
    by the time I was I wasn't
the best thing little girls can be
I never was
could never be
good or godly
pure or spotless
    what my family wanted
    or that's what I believed

when I was 18
they said
I could be born again as a virgin
    as if I was the reason
    my innocence died

repent, take a pledge
buy a ring, commit to Jesus
no more sex before marriage
don't even think about it
forget all that happened
before this moment
celebrate celibacy by birthing virginity
give us control of your body

no questions
especially not about
   sexuality or consent
   pleasure or pain
   how 11-year-old virgins get pregnant

if the Holy Spirit's breath
on Mary's neck
   smelled like theirs
   on mine

Super Glue

we broke the Virgin Mary
the one our catholic grandpa made
surely an unforgiveable sin

snapped her neck right in half
it was an accident
playing with people
and animals in the manger
moving them around
re-arranging the hay
re-creating the stories
we heard on Sunday
acting out scenes from movies
that had nothing to do with Jesus

we were kids
bored, imaginative
counting down the days
trying to make sense
of the world we lived in

it was scary
holding her belly in one hand
her head in another
believing we were in really big trouble
life as we knew it eternally over

a small stabbing pain in my palm
a piece of her pressed deep into my skin

suddenly the expectation of Christmas
felt more like the agony of Good Friday

as we super glued Mary back together
I used tweezers to pull her flesh from mine

this year feels a lot like that year
afraid my brokenness is breaking others
will the body I hold in my left hand
ever rejoin the heart held in my right

like creation
always on the cusp of war
on the brink of paradise
one breath could make or break us all

strong
like a young mother
giving birth in a countryside stable
cradling him
holding fear
rocking worry
swaddling hopes
nursing dreams

the lines between breaking and loving
are especially thin

like star light and super glue
binding us back together

Tradition Tells Me

epiphany is coming
I don't see it

they say
we are not supposed to
not until it comes

magi traveling
   a different way
   a dangerous way
   a daring way
following a light
most cannot fathom
bringing gifts most cannot afford
to a baby many claim to love
but whose love they will not hold

for if they held it
they would have to drop
   their weapons
   and plots of revenge
let go of
   control
release
   power

I want to believe it's out there
that I'd follow the stars
if I could see them

tradition tells me
we keep missing it

Breaking In

I was in 5th grade the second time
our house was broken into
we went away for memorial day
when we came home
   the dog ran right inside

it took a minute
to register the back door
was wide open before we ever opened it

   televisons, videos games
   my mercedes benz baseball cap
   dwayne wayne sunglasses

gone

but the worst thing stolen
a sense of safety and innocence
that was pretty shaky to begin with

being the oldest and most protective
I huddled us kids like a mother hen
for weeks we all slept in one twin size bed

what if they came back
knew when we were home alone
did they look in drawers
snoop through closets
read diaries
rummage through comic book collections

who were they
   people we knew who knew we were away
   family, friends, strangers

did they touch our toothbrushes
use the toilet
eat food from the fridge

I hadn't thought about this
for a very long time
this morning I woke with it
heavy on my mind
wondering why

it comes to me

it's the one-year anniversary
of insurrection
the connection
the intense feelings
of vulnerability, violation
fear, helplessness
the self-righteous rage of privileged whiteness

racism, nationalism
domestic christian terrorism breaking in
breaking down doors, bashing windows
stealing figurines, sculptures, podiums
swinging from the rafters
throwing fire extinguishers, profanities
flying flags of hatred, waving weapons
brandishing threats while shirtless
wearing horns
claiming to be shamans
feet on someone's desk
lighting up a cigarette
taking a shit in someone's office

snapping selfies
tweeting
calling home bragging to mom and dad

   who were they
   our fathers, grandfathers,
   husbands, sons, brothers, uncles
   our mothers, daughters, sisters, wives
   our pastors, co-workers
   next-door neighbors were there too

suddenly
I'm 10 years old again
afraid, unsafe, unsure again
in my home
in my country
in the world

it dawns on me
today is also epiphany
another type of breaking in
   of goodness, innocence
   grace, magical wisdom
awesome brilliance
wise ones traveling by star light
to celebrate, commemorate
god's presence among us
emmanuel now and forever with us

slowly soaking
seeping in
realization
revelation
even on the bleakest, hardest days
light and life break in

miraculously, mysteriously
through the least and last expected
ones repeatedly rejected
through tiny cracks, small spaces
places we forgot and neglected
hammered shut
to keep the robbers out
when we were kids

here and now breaking in
not with violence and force
but with gentleness and invitation
hope comes
we hear them say
will you join me
in illuminating a different way

Clowning Around

as a kid
   I thought every good parade
had candy
I hated though
that it was thrown by clowns
clowns have always scared me

   I thought parades
were for patriotic holidays
or when your sports team
won the championship

   I thought parades
were always on paved streets
with floats, marching bands
musicians in matching uniforms
instruments in hand
people coming early
to get their lawn chair
in the front row

so, I was a bit confused
when a preacher said
Palm Sunday was a parade

where was the candy
who were the clowns
why
what were they celebrating
how did floats get

   p
u
and
d
  o
     w
        n

those dirt country roads

what about the band
what instruments could they play
with palms in their hands

  maybe the problem
was my lacking imagination
maybe I couldn't see celebration
because I learned about Easter first
like I couldn't experience
the depth of Good Friday
because we speed past death
to get right to resurrection rebirth

was Jesus on the donkey the clown
clowning around
clowning the crowd
not the ones
on the sidewalk waving palms
or walking beside him
but the ones a little farther back
watching as skeptics
judging eyes
from a state sponsored surveillance seat
what is this guy doing now

  maybe the music
wasn't a song at all

but the message of it all
all the production
symbolism
over the top parallelism
processing, politicalizing
meant to challenge powers
principalities, local localities
their parade permits
authorized routes
who we are to worship, adore
what we are to follow, revere

what constitutes life
justifies death
fills our hearts with sorrow
moves us to rejoice
pulls us to action
pushes us to silence

what we choose to celebrate
what we consider sweet

candy or mercy
tootsie rolls or suffering
charm pops or grace
smarties or violence
laffy taffy or redemption

Unleavened

it's hard to swallow
unleavened bread
fruit of the vine
awareness death is close
coming closer
empire is risING
getting StRoNgEr
tightening its grip on power

the realization everything
will soon change forever
reality will forever be altered
his betrayer was invited
given a seat at the table

how dare he be invited
show up at the table
knowing those hands
so resembling mine
hold the same doubts
temptations as I…
…I wonder, why?

   what is the lesson
this night comes every year
yet the experience is never lessened
by time or remembrance

we do this
in remembrance of him
but why

the one who shows us
   how to live and why to die
   when to share a meal with friends
with kin
even with ones
who will trade your life for a dime
he pours it all out
that we might know how
to feast on presence
inhale the sweet
and bitter fragrance of the vine

the bread
it's still
so hard
to swallow

Our Feet

breakfast was over
there wasn't much to clean up
she ate mostly cottage cheese and peaches
drank just a small glass of juice
after rinsing the bowl in the sink
   I asked did she think
there was anything else she needed

she paused, sighed
shyly asked if I'd clip her toenails
   I stopped, cringed
said I'll be right back

went to gather what I thought I'd need
courage, a towel, clippers, a file
   I sat down at her feet
that were resting on a stool covered
in green velvet-like fabric
similar to that of her rocking chair
gently pulling off her socks
   I realized
we didn't know what we were in for

a few minutes later returning
with a plastic tub
filled with warm soapy water
a washcloth, lotion, pair of rubber gloves

her feet like her hands
the rest of her body
nearing 90 years old
her toenails discolored, overgrown

coated in a thick fungus
that smelled so bad

my stomach was turning
17-year-old me thinking
    I'd rather be anywhere but here

this is gross, disgusting
loved her more than anyone, anything
this was more than I wanted to do
she knew that, too
it was more than she wanted to ask of me
but her feet were tired, sore
her toenails causing so much pain, discomfort
her pride as strong as her stubbornness

pushing past the urge to gag
    I knew it was an honor
to be trusted with this task
taking a deep breath
began my work
overly cautious
so afraid of hurting her
cutting or accidently shaming her

    I don't remember conversation
between us
certainly not connecting this
to anything sacred
like Jesus washing the feet of his disciples
shortly before his death
after years of walking in that direction

such intimacy
cleansing the spirit
even more than the flesh
causing such uneasiness

bringing insecurities to the surface
crossing lines of social acceptability
familial responsibility
stretching personal boundaries

   I wasn't thinking about Peter
questioning Jesus or Jesus saying
"maybe not now, later
you'll understand what I'm doing"

an early spring morning
that much I do remember
warm enough for my grandpa
to open the balcony door

the feel of the breeze
sweet scent of wet grass
stench of cigarette smoke rising
from the sidewalk below
expressway noise behind us

a few months later
they moved to a nursing home
a few months after that
my great-grandma died
a broken hip turned pneumonia

   I wasn't with her
for that last labored breath
but present
for many of the days and nights
leading in that direction
   holding her hand
   rubbing her feet
   praying
   singing together
   listening helplessly to her cries

as pain, fear, ultimately death
took over

realizing she'd been heading that direction
since that morning I clipped her toenails
washed, dried, massaged her feet
with discontinued Avon lotion

   I didn't understand then
but now I know
this moment in time changes me
comforts, sustains
guides, convicts
cleanses, refreshes
dare I even say
it saves me
and all of us
who risk
letting bare feet
be washed this day
by one we will soon betray
who is still trying to help us
understand what we're doing

Patent Pending

we celebrate again
   after three days gone
Jesus back from the dead

this year
struggling with celebration
not feeling hosannas and jubilation

maybe it's the pain of the world
graves in Ukraine and Sudan
tombs in Haiti and Gaza
migrants huddled around the world
waiting
for gates to be
o p e n e d
barbed wires to be
~rolled~ away

a country on egg shells
as a man fills our baskets
with patriotic bibles
propped up by
shards of broken glass
hidden in fake green grass

wondering how many will buy
take up these weapons
lamenting lives lost
families destroyed when bridges

c
  o
    l
     l
      a
       p
        s
         e

from all the cargo we carry

maybe it's the state of the church
realizing the place that taught me rebirth
has no idea what it means
seems unable, unwilling to see
they do not hold
the patent on resurrection

maybe it's the position of my life
hope pending
suspended between
   not there
   not quite here
neither caterpillar
     nor butterfly
out of the grave
not fully alive

Smirk

I spent last Christmas Eve
   in the ICU
   at the bedside of my mother
kept alive by a ventilator
even though I'd bought
a new festive red sweater
I skipped church because
celebrating birth
seemed both cruel and impossible

17 years ago
I was the patient
   hospitalized for the 20-something-th
   and final time
for depression so deep
I only longed to die

after an experience
that still feels unbelievable
sitting at a metal desk
in front of a safety glass mirror
seeing life in a clearer way
from a barricaded window
pouring my heart out on paper
   poems and prayers
indistinguishable

telling the psychiatrist
   tomorrow is Maundy Thursday
   I'd like to be home for supper
   have time to buy
   something new to wear
   to church on Easter

with a smirk he asked
   if I agree to discharge you,
   what do you possibly think you're going to do?

with all the hope I could gather
   I said, *learn to live or die trying*

months after death came so close
my mother is home
breathing, healing, walking
talking, loving, trusting

years after depression loosened its grip
I've settled in to my own body and being
learning, finding
exploring, doing
what the doctors said I never would

on this day of resurrection
my mother and I sit together
in the sanctuary that brought us together
where I first encountered resurrection
in a new bold blue sweater
having discovered so much about faith
   facing the impossible
   rolling stones
   releasing sorrows
that seem too permanent to move

imagining that doctor no longer smirking
but smiling as I tell him
   I'm living
   haven't died yet trying

Sacramental Supplements

they're all wrong everything is grace

Homesick

   like my great-grandmother's
soft talcum powder scented hands
upon my cheeks I miss her
our separation a constant source
of pain and longing

many are those who say she is past her prime
her glory days have gone and died
ain't no hope of resurrection
focusing on poverty and blight
scandal and corruption

her babies have joined the angry masses
flocking to the outer rings
in search of opportunity and promise
the gifts those suburbs bring
   but abandoning the center
only weakens the circle

like my great-grandmother's
soft talcum powder scented hands
upon my cheeks brought warmth and comfort
for her calloused hands upon my soul
   I am healed
   I am whole
the first to love me unconditionally
to accept me just as I am
without asking for credentials
or references
she gave me a chance
no judgment of my past
trusted me enough to reveal
both her pride and her sorrow

on the river walk
she rocked me as steamboats went by
in the ren cen lifted me to reach
and touch the sky

on woodward and adams
she put a new song in my heart
we are all god's children
all deserve a pair of shoes

in cass corridor she showed me
what every child need know
about love and forgiveness
the high cost of hatred

in the back hall
of an old brick building on vernor
the power of students teaching teachers
lessons that can't be learned from a book
or hiding behind steel bleachers
   vandalized abandoned schools
   chalkboards stained with scribbled rules
symbolize the nature of her education
still separate, still unequal
one city's lack reflects the nation's

she led me through del ray
the reality of ecological disaster
how one's zip code increases
the likelihood of exposure to disease
   deadly air, dirty drinking water

southfield, greenfield
all her fields depict the collision
of redlining and redevelopment
prosperity for one
relocation for another

in a camp by campus martius
the power of a community
committed to saving one of their own
it is too cold for you to be on the street
   let us take you in
   you need not be alone

a choir of children singing at the fountain
we shall move this mountain
lifting the value of the arts
the danger of balancing budgets at their expense
they've more than done their part

oh sweet belle isle, nature's glorious gift
evidence that conservation and preservation
are needs and not some hippie liberal wish

everyday I pray the winds of change
steer me back to her
wrestling with the guilt of leaving her

she is more
than some city that took me in
   my pulse and heartbeat
   my passion within
the reason I live
not in need of charity
   atonement or salvation
she is due
   respect, compassion
      a loud roaring standing ovation

I was reborn
baptized in a city
the country would soon forget
embraced by her beauty
miraculously made whole

enlightened by her suffering
awakened to a call

   like my great-grandmother's hands
offering a word
Detroit's hands deliver a message
rivers of justice cannot flow
lest we
        break
        the
        dams

Quality over Quantity

two sacraments
   for one grandmother
seven
   for another
in some sanctuaries
   none
     whatsoever

I'm living like
they're all wrong
everything is grace
   sacred
   holy

Healing

what is healing?

necessary, supernatural
forced, manipulation
a means of control, a promise
a prize, a show

what is healing?

when a preacher proclaims
your symptom is a test
your sickness a demon
your very being an incarnation
of satan himself
your existence proof
evil is alive and walking among us

what is healing?

the hands of a self-appointed
questionably anointed apostle
upon your head
pressing hard
        HARDER
the weight of his power
upon you
crushing your soul
   to exorcise sin

what is healing?

a group of strangers
disguised as church leaders

hovering behind you
one with a white sheet
ChOmPiNg at the bit
for you to fall out
out, come out
they pray
in english
and unknown tongues they pray

what is healing?

praying the gay away
the depression
shame
sorrow away
demanding you throw your pills
therapist's phone number
girlfriend away

what is healing?

the courage to stand up and say
no, stop
the strength to run away
fast and far away

I know more
what healing is not

still I've got a feeling
that healing is
   sacred moments
   holy encounters
   freedom
   cutting of cords
   releasing secrets

breaking chains
   birthing dreams

the entirety of our lives
from the minute
the womb births open
   pushing us
      into the world
until that day the earth breaks forth
receiving us
    back
into her arms

Smile

she taught me Jesus smiled
   I can too
to open the blinds
let sunshine in
   I can shine too

   her smile sings in my heart
as living and loving keep us apart
walking the bay of another coast
under moonlight and dark
   her smile connects
those parts of my journey
marked by polar extremes
unimaginable miles
seeming too far
s-t-r-e-t-c-h-e-d to be related

not related by blood
but by water
sweeter than juice
flavored by pine needles
petoskey stones, pickerel lakes
warmed by the sunlight
she invited me to welcome in
all those years ago
when I was just a child
learning to open the blinds
   to not be afraid
   to smile

Lois

blessed are the life bearers
Eve, Lilith, Naamah
all their daughters
   for theirs is the soil of earth
      the garden of our birth

blessed are the birds
bearing olive branches
guiding us from the waters of the womb
leading us home
when the flooding retreats
   for they know the way to peace

blessed are the laboring hands
sowing
scattering seeds
understanding sand, silt, clay
that even rocks can produce
   for they are the dreamers of revolutionary dreams

blessed are the hearts
greener than thumbs
planting flowers and trees alike
offering sustenance
enhancing the beauty
we all long to see
   for they are makers of miracles

blessed are the patient farmers
teaching their crafts
sharing rakes, shovels, plows
knowledge of sun and light
morning and night

what thrives in the shade
   for they are cultivating the future

blessed are the gardens
encompassed by hundreds of acres
and those nestled in small corner lots
where deer and fox
the unhoused and uninvited
find welcome and rest
   for they thrive
      on the power of belonging

blessed are the gardeners
making soul filling meals
from the harvest
gently reminding
today's plate holds all we need
neither yesterday nor tomorrow
should cause us angst or worry
   for they are the embodiment
      of here and now
         now and not yet

blessed are the feet that stand still
walking bare
playing in puddles
praying in the mud
dancing in the rain
baking cakes from the dirt
decorating them with stones
   for they know
      what is holy is also messy
         broken things can be mended
            when we simply tend to them

blessed are the warm smiles
of protectors and advocates

caring for air, land, sea
with the same tenderness
extended to blisters and callouses
who recognize the tree of life
is eternal and regenerating
holding the roots of our calling
    for they have spent generations nurturing them

blessed are we
gathered within these gates
committing the ashes
of a life lived so wondrously well
leaving a legacy ripe with joy
modeling how to experience
grief, loss, disappointment, pain
without being overcome by it

blooming with hospitality
radiating justice
exuding mercy
love like an endless basket
of loaves and fish
fresh fruits, rare cheeses
strange mushrooms
    perhaps a piece of tofu

showing us
a different way to tell
when it's time
for living and dying
loving and trying
laughing and crying
learning and yearning
hoping and healing

blessed are we
beloveds of Lois

    for she is
        still inviting us
            to sing in the garden
                to enjoy this feast
                    she has prepared
                        from garden to table

Head in the Clouds

since we are surrounded
by such a great cloud of witnesses

what if it isn't a great cloud
  but a strong circle
what if we aren't surrounded
  but included
  loved
  supported

what if the saints aren't simply those
who've gone on ahead
  but those right here now
    standing before us
    leading us on
    following behind us
    pushing us forward
    walking beside us
    holding our hand
    steadying our stride

what if they're not solely
  witnesses to our lives
    but participants

what if they're not just watching
  from a distance
but joyfully living
the journey with us
  lighting our collective way

Inquire Within

I went to church on Sunday
heard a sermon that stirred me
music that moved me
prayers that pulled me
   closer to the holy
an unexpected blessing keeps me
will not let me go

near the end of the service
they called him forward
   a man who has for years
tenderly tended to the sacristy
the little room behind the platform
like a pantry for all things holy
keeping it clean, stocked, organized
keeping track of supplies
ordering more when
   quantities get low

they thanked him
honored him
named him the official sacristan
then we all joined in to bless him
   as the keeper of holy things

that moment keeps coming back to me

what if we all accepted this position
applied it to our daily living
   like we ask for daily bread
holding all things as holy
keeping all things wholly sacred

keeping ourselves
   enemies
   friends
as beloved

keeping our dreams
   fears
   laughter and tears
   bodies and beings
as the beauty the creator created

keeping confident
   and proud when those loud voices
   come to tell us
      we were born sinfully bad
needing to sacrifice our flesh
to keep our spirits pure

keeping focus on the places
torn by war and violence
   on the people dying
   before our collective eyes
the ones they tell us are
   expendable
   damaged
   collateral

keeping sight on the powerful
and power
   those working to maintain it
secure it
limit who has access to it

keeping attentive to the earth
where it's burning faster than it's turning
where governments are keeping watch
over borders by night and by day

where sheep are slaughtered
little lambs not allowed to play

keeping love like watches keep time
    like lovers keep time in a bottle
    like truckers keep a foot on the throttle

keeping grace like grandmas keep trinkets
    like little kids keep secrets
    like we keep keepsakes in the junk drawer

keeping peace like the light we keep on
all the things we keep not knowing what for

keeping faith like we keep spare change
in a jar on the counter
    like we keep memories in our hearts
    like we keep vigil as dear ones pass on
    and pass over

keeping joy like we keep hope alive
    like we keep stories in our minds
    like we keep watching old movies
        over and over

keeping sacraments just long enough
    to bless, release them
keeping rituals just tight enough
    to loose them
keeping the shelves just full enough
    to feed them
all the hungry people in the world

keeping forgiveness and liberation
    instead of rules and tradition
keeping gospels of good news
    not books of laws and discipline

keeping imagination sharp and active
   like a box of two-edged colored pencils
keeping scripture and mystery
as guides and stencils

keeping altars and forests clutter free
keeping baptismal fonts and rivers flowing
clear of blocks and debris

keeping open to miracles
   possibilities
   invitations
to the ways god is calling
to the signs all around us
   saying, *sacristans wanted*

o, the blessings we could be
when we all agree to be keepers
keeping all things holy

Quarters

two quarters every Sunday
one for the offering plate
another the coffee hour donation bowl
like a token inserted into a magical machine
pushing out a nutty donut
and a styrofoam cup filled with
   syrupy sweet red punch

my great-grandpa would say with a wink
keep your quarter, I got you covered
   felt like winning the lotto
in a religion denouncing gambling
making it more exciting

after church we played Liverpool Rum
if my great-grandma saw me struggling
to lay down a hand
she'd smile while flashing me a card
mouthing the question, *is this what you need*
even when it wasn't the ace
I was waiting for
feeling like a queen with a full heart

with the deck STackED against me
someone wanted me to win

For the Day You Baptize a Book

not a cleansing
because you're already clean
not a purification
because you've always been pure

not a new cover
or second edition
or a reprint of the original

but a remembering
an honoring
of every letter
   every word
   every line
   every page
   every chapter
in this story and the next
   every scar
   every scribble
   every edit
   every typo
   every rejection
each and every
   thank you and not yet

may it all be blessed
and healed
may it be healing
and blessing
to you and
to those holding and telling
their own tales of living and learning

wondering and knowing
sinking and floating

to those waiting and wanting
questioning if and where they belong

may this book
like your calling
be belonging
as it continues flowing
like water from a public not for profit fountain
that's divine and not over zealous
spiritual and not fundamentally religious
holy in a wholistic kinda way
sacred like mystery not certainty
sacramental without assigning authority

pouring out grace
   or love
   or kindness
   or compassion
   or creativity if that's what is missing
   or forgiveness
   or acceptance
   or direction
   or permission for leaving
if that is what you're needing
it's never what a pastor says you are lacking

baptism is receiving
the nourishment you seek
as often as you go seeking

as ordinary as a cup of warm tap water
a bedtime shower
a puddle in the driveway after the rain
the leaky faucet that keeps you awake

a community pool
a sprinkler
a stream
a pond
a river
a lake
ocean waves singing your name

baptism is celebrating your being
creation matching the rhythm of your breathing

renewal never ending
energy ever bubbling
guiding you where you are going

baptism is trusting who you are
baptism is knowing where you are going

Daily Bread

    some mornings I awake
begin without a word
sure that yesterday's portion will sustain me

    others I rise
seeking a week's supply
fearing famine of nourishment and time

    today I am hungry
ask to be fed
give us this day our daily bread

Fragile Things

I used to fear fragile things
walking slowly past them
like I did as a kid
in a fancy gift shop
once I touched a glass Christmas ornament
my grandmother screamed
don't, you'll break it!
for years wouldn't go near
anything I might accidentally break

tip-toeing around all this time
has taught me lessons
I never learned in a classroom
or from my grandmother's high pitch warnings

fragile isn't to be feared
but respected
not avoided
but approached with care
   awe, wonder

somethings do sometimes break
the real question
what do we do with the brokenness?

holding life in my hands
unafraid
all the fragile, broken
chipped, sharp pieces
not ready to
   throw them away
pondering new ways of
   putting them together

Appetite Change

my early memories of communion
don't include receiving it
but watching with fascination
Ms. Francis and Ms. Marva
preparing it in the sacristy
doing their methodist magic
gracefully filling little cups
   with juice
gently hand tearing small pieces
   of bread
careful where I stood
not wanting to be seen
in a space I didn't belong

around the same time
I remember longingly watching
the priest place a wafer
on my grandparents' tongue during mass
another place I didn't belong

can't recall the first time I took it
but once I did
I wanted it again and again
wasn't interested in solving the mystery
just experiencing it
being part of it
included, grounded, rooted in it

first Sunday of every month
walking toward a table
I believed was set for me
imagine the pain of learning it wasn't
a gradual lesson not a single moment

still I would go take it
no longer sweet or filling
it was bitter and left me searching

leaving the church
of my birth and becoming
losing more than a building
I surrendered my credentials
and my place of belonging
I'm a better me than I was back then
stronger and whole in deeper ways
I couldn't even pray for back then

but I wasn't completely over
my Sunday cravings for ritual
the right amount of tradition
familiar music, a passing peace
despite the yearnings I stayed away
because I felt my appetite changing

as a child I loved blue cheese
as an adult won't touch it
as a child I thought coffee was disgusting
as an adult can't get enough of it
   still love the bread
but not the crust attached to it
   still love the juice
but not the crumbs dropped into it
I accepted living without it

then I met this graceful baker
gentle nectar maker
like those old sacristan magicians
I watched them from a distance
not only the plate and the cup
but the table
they were so intentional in creating

safe, accessible, intersectional
personal, radical, sacramental
invitational without persuasion
no coercion or coded expectations
queers and queerly beloveds
stuffed foxes
sloths wearing tortoise shells
and penguins
all savoring communion

the raisin bread gluten free
the drink not too sweetened
help me to understand my appetite change

  if it's kneaded by exclusion
baked with power
served with reservations
by those who've met requirements for ordination

  if it's picked with shame
ripened by control
poured with judgement
I don't want it
no longer have an appetite
for what others believe I don't deserve

it was never really about sacraments
but the connection they created
an authentic seat at a table
I had to wander a bit
  and
in my wandering I found it
a place at the belonging table

Synchronizing

let's go chase the moon together

All Seems Lost

when all seems lost
imagine for a moment
that it is
what's the first thing
you go looking for

    a blanket to cover the flames
when the hydrants are dry
    a boulder to stand on
until the flooding subsides
    a magic carpet to fly
rescuing everyone
the birds and bears left behind

    an evacuation plan
when hurricane winds blow
bringing monsoon rains
embers and ash
destruction in the path

    a safe harbor when storms
and hateful legislations pass
as protections for the vulnerable are ~~slashed~~
like tree tops
when tornadoes whirl through

    a steady structure
when earthquakes shake the foundation
further eroding the s e p a r a t i o n
of church-and-state

    a circle to invite others into
    an opening created to stay

even as it ex-----pands
and closes to protect
the most at risk from isolation

    a pair of gloves for frost bit fingers
    a bottle of water when heat domes linger
    a shovel when snow falls
faster and heavier than the land
and rooftops can hold
    a bag of salt when ice makes
every s.t.e.p. more perilous

    a mask when air pollution
viruses and unchecked lies
roam the skies
seeking home in human bodies
and MaNiPuLaTeD minds

    a balm for curing sickness
    a smooth stone to press against our palms
when it's time to let go
    a wise one to help us know the difference
    a gentleness to guide our grief
    a compass to navigate our anger

    a place to align
that puts people
        over
        party lines
public health
        over
        profits
where there are no aisles
    or
sides
only pillows made of softness and joy

a microphone that's never turned on
because the lowest voices
are eternally amplified

   a key that unlocks gates
   a feather to bring down walls
   a whisper that opens borders
   an hour glass filled with butterflies
when time moves too slow
or speeds on by

   a song that like a siren
will stop evil in its tracks
   a melody that makes this war the last
   a tune that turns dropping bombs
into
fa
   ll
      ing sacks
packed with toys for children
baskets of warm bread
fresh berries and sweet peaches
for mothers to feed them

   a notebook of words
that rhyme not with sounds
but with meaning
pulsing with hope
metered with healing

   a ticket to find your kindred
   a DJ to bring the beat
as you turn up your volume
   a parquet floor to dance on
as you dance upon injustice
under glittery disco balls

rainbow confetti
exPLODing from the rafters

   a mountain to climb
as fears are rising
   a cave for hiding and birthing
   a green valley for resting and dreaming

   a forest
to bathe in sunshine and beaming
while all the wounds are mending

   a garden
to plant all the feelings
seeding resurrection
after we've buried the dying

   a harvest
of the mundane
and extraordinary things growing

we once could only imagine
when all seemed lost
and far beyond our finding

Truth Be Told

I told the truth today
it cost me $19
even the cashier told me
I should have just kept walking
when I waved my hand
to call him over

in a world
where lies are served like bread
spread like butter
eaten without question
ingested without care of consequence
   televised
   advertised
   packaged
   sold in bulk

whatever it cost
I needed truth to matter

Hold On

yesterday I was so sure
our hands are able to hold
multiple things
even and especially things
commonly considered to be in opposition
like joy and sorrow
celebration and lamentation

I'd like to say
I learned this from church
but watching from a protective distance
as they celebrate
   and proclaim their joy
I wonder where the sorrow
   and lamenting rest
I already hear the scolding
just let us have our moment

it must be there
below
the
surface
work done out of sight
behind
     the scenes
approved in blocks
what's done in committee will redeem us
  right?

this church that filled my heart with love
for god and the world
did not teach me to hold
   complexities and simplicities

    soft tenderness and harsh injustice
    hope and despair
    rejoicing and wailing
    lamenting, waiting and celebrating
in tension
with equal care and attention
they told me I had to choose

the true teachers were time and rejection
the strangers I've met in exile turned eden
the ones I now call friends and family
who reached out today
in a multitude of ways

asking sweetly
how are you dear one?
thinking of you.
are you okay?
as they dance in the joy of this moment
while continually keeping silent
on the sorrows that brought them there

my heart is there
and it's here
in this life I'm building
one
    slow
brick
    at
    a
    time
a queer labor of self-love
out in the daylight for all
even the skeptics and scoffers
to see

I'm holding space
like I'm holding all this emotion
carefully, prayerfully
with two hands
and honest reflection

still sure about what
our hands
        can hold
wishing it wasn't so

h
  e
    a
      v
        y

Things I Can Trust Right Now

in a world of shifting vaults
shaking earth
quaking doubts
here are things
I can trust right now

the wind blowing off the water
   landing on my face
the footprints my sneakers
   leave in the snow
the mud that paints the soul
the ageless rocks
   and softening sand
the gentle raindrop in my hand
the blue birds singing
   while swinging on red vines
     standing out among brown branches
the seagulls perched on power lines

the curiosity flowing
   and wonder growing
the art of unknowing
the trail I'm walking
the future I'm creating
the signs marking the path
the stickers on the bathroom wall
the hearts etched into the stall
the support of wobbly railings
the rest of unlevel benches

the barista pouring my lavender latte
   with pronouns
     proudly pinned to their apron

the neighbor ringing the bell
   right before delivering
   a basket of fresh peaches
the stranger in the store
   handing me a coupon saying
   maybe you need this

the smell of bacon for Saturday brunch
the conversation I had over lunch
   with an old friend
the courage to try again
the audacity to begin
the monsters gone
   from under the bed
the rocking chair in the corner
the silence of Sunday morning
the new pack of brightly colored pens
   resting on a soft covered journal
the last few pages asking to be filled

the Lucille Clifton poems
   and Mary Oliver essays
   on the ottoman
the invitation to read them
   one
   letter
   at
   a
   time

the watch that hasn't worked in years
   sitting beautifully on my wrist
the gentle giver who gifted it
the reminder that broken is beautiful
the smell of spring and clean laundry
the feel of a freshly laundered blanket
   draping over me

the first sip of coffee
   from the mug she made me
   and filled with chocolates
the last drop of chamomile tea
blueberries and licorice
the dog sleeping
   burrowed deeply into my hip

memories of the life I've lived
and the dreams I've dreamt
the ones that came true
   and those that keep me spent

the love I've found
the one I lost
   searching for
     my own heart
the way it stopped beating
   right before I found
     the story's meaning

my instinct
the voice calling
   come along
   let's go chase the moon together
the stars guiding our way
the sun that just might rise
another day

Left Wondering

taught to believe
strangeness in the heart is a warming
more now like a warning

   don't get too close to that fire
   be warry of those flames
   you left to heal
   to live
   you are healing so beautifully
   living so wildly wonderfully well
   it hasn't been easy
   you're doing it so well

the longer I'm
out of the closet
the more I understand
the wardrobe of ways
church never let me in

rejection is uniquely enacted
restoration too
has its own threads
patterns

   you are right to wonder

what does it look like
for those rejected
with no interest in returning
for those who are discerning
totally uncertain
those told their files are missing
locked in a storage room

only dead people
   hold the keys to unlocking

wherever we are
or plan on going
all our rejection deserves acknowledging
apology

I'm still wondering
what restoration means
is it just about orders and credentials
what about relationships
shared humanity
personal dignity
denominational integrity
practical things like pensions
   livelihoods
     debt release

I'm still wondering and probably will always be

when I'm not out
in the water
or the woods
living
loving
moving
being

penning poems
telling stories
that on Sundays
are still
sometimes
called
a sermon

That's When

when what feeds you
   also starves you
when what keeps you alive
   also keeps you from living
that's when
you have nothing to lose

when you give up a sure meal
   wanting to create a sustainable harvest
when you disconnect from the cord
   dying to breathe on your own
that's when
intuition will guide you

when you wander from the well
   thirsty yet drained from judgement
when you seek new sources of sustenance
   uncertain yet expectant
that's when
the spirit provides

Learning to Walk in the Dark

born in a city ablaze with light
magnifying pollution factories projected
racism embedded in the assembly line
local elections
school classrooms
church sanctuaries
and biblical interpretations

raised in a white family
plagued by poverty
and a cataclysm of isms

envious when others speak
of the good ole days
when they knew their mothers
would stand on the front porch
calling them home
when the street lights came on
my street's lights were often out
could stay out all night
with no one noticing
                        I
was gone

grew up thinking
every city had a devil's night
fires intentionally set
ushering in Halloween with flames
illuminating the sky
like fireworks on the 4th of July

walked alone
to the bus stop each morning

before sunrise
afraid of the dangers lurking
in burned out buildings
overgrown shrubs

walked alone
to church on Sundays
sometimes Mondays, Wednesdays, Thursdays
careful of broken concrete
stray dogs
all the things I was taught to fear

it was only when I was out of the city
away from the busy
disconnected from
the overburdened electrical grid
that my perspective began to shift
each summer
lifted
up
to my great grandparents' cottage on the lake
three hours and light years away

walked alone
on the beach to the rhythm of the waves
in the woods
through pines
  oaks
    maples
  cedars

on railroad tracks
into town for ice cream
bought with the change
grandpa gave me for changing light bulbs
in the red shed that kept the shuffleboard cues

at dawn and at dusk
without a d
        r
        o
        p
of fear in my heart
or my head

in the sand at 4:00 AM
gazing at stars
an epiphany

was it the factory
that produced my family's dysfunction
   or something more industrial

what is the source
of that foul stench
overtaking the city on hot summer days

why am I the only white kid in class now
why is everyone at church white like me
who really sets those October fires

how did I become afraid of the dark
who said bad things don't happen in the light
why does the painting of Jesus with porcelain skin
blue eyes and blond hair scare me

what if everything they've taught me is wrong
   darkness the enemy
   light and white the pinnacle of humanity
   dark and black what we should avoid
      seek not
         to be

like the fine line of powder
on the *etch a sketch* screen
it became so clear to me
    the way we associate shapes our reality
it's time to rewrite our vocabulary

learning to walk in the dark
by this I mean

steering from the path my ancestors paved for me

releasing the fears others birthed in me

understanding the world in colors
    beyond my imagination
in concepts
deeper
than historic indoctrinations
with words outside
racist glossaries of explanation

Asked to Define Success

writing
with the audacity
   of a slickly dressed street preacher
delusional
about power of the tongue
and goodness of the message
liberating hearts from threat
   of eternal judgement
releasing ridiculous love
casting hell
into its own fake lake of fire
heaven
   roaming
among us

Card for Coming Out

down from the video store
just before the donut place
was a little brick building
one side a pharmacy
the other a Hallmark shop

it always smelled like
cinnamon and Christmas
warm like a fire kindling
soft like an afghan
on my grandmother's sofa
no matter the season

I felt free and festive
walking the greeting card aisles
an entrance to a world
of creativity and curiosity
a colorful card for all reasons
an appropriate note for every occasion

what if there'd been one then
for coming out day
celebrating being queer
having the strength
courage to say
for all to hear
this is me
who I am
what I like
who I love
all I want to be

maybe it wouldn't have been so hard
I wouldn't have been so alone
the closet would have opened sooner
felt more like a birthday
less like a funeral

what if there were cards
that fell from the sky
every time someone
smiles in the mirror
tries on pronouns
puts on what they really want to wear
cuts off or grows out their hair

what if there were cards for families
inspiring them to love their children
siblings and friends
a few poetic lines of affirmation
to stop them drawing lines
of hate and condemnation

what if there were cards for schools
teachers, churches, preachers
neighbors, strangers
politicians weaponizing gender
sporting competitions
angry men at basketball games
pride parades
carrying big bloody signs
warning about hell
other false dangers
    inviting them to reimagine
      deadly positions

what if there were cards
the kind that sing when you open them
proclaiming the beauty and joy of

  the L
    the G
    the B
     the T
      the Q
       the I
        the A
         the +
          the 2
the queer magic and glory of just being you

the miraculous honor
transformative power
of someone coming out to you

I want to create a world
where every sidewalk
is a rainbow lined hall
with glitter sprinkling from the ceiling
marking the ever-unraveling journey
of living and being

personalized cards
for every emotion and feeling
each step
milestone of coming out and into
graciously greeting
warmly welcoming who we are
and are created to be

  I write these cards for you

Ready or Not

I'm not really ready for hope
but if you must send it
wrap it in the fading comic section
from Sunday's newspaper

secure it with duct tape
use minty dental floss as ribbon
to hold it together

take it to the post office
wait without complaining in the long line
thank the clerk for their hard work
don't order anyone with a blank face to smile
add extra postage to make sure it arrives

   I'm not really ready for hope
but if you must share it
don't make it fluffy and soft

describe the time you bashed
your toe on a hard rock
your nail fell off and it hurt like hell

don't make it so sugary sweet
that my teeth shiver
leave in the bitter
mix in the memory of losing your gloves
in the coldest of winters
invite me to feel the frost bite on your fingers

   I'm not really ready for hope
but if you must sing it

make it a symphony
not simply a song

you're not a composer?
challenge yourself to learn
before you dare call yourself a teacher
tell me your brokenness
before you claim yourself a healer

  I'm not really ready for hope
but if you must promote it
be honest about why
it's in such short supply

how like resilience and egg prices
we exploit it
use it to soothe our guilt
denying the ways
we harm others
while glorifying their survival
    knowing how doesn't mean I should have to

  I'm not really ready for hope
but if you must explain it
remind me of Jim and the crows
how 1619 and 2008
January 6th weren't that long ago

wade through the muddy waters of roe
back alley abortions
the young woman who died last week
when doctors wouldn't help her miscarry
for threat of being sued

speak to the black women
who ran polling locations in cities
throughout this country

returning home to texts
about being taken back to the plantation
ballot boxes caught on fire
bomb threats in strategically chosen places
don't let me forget
dare me to remember

   I'm not really ready for hope
but if you must uplift it
don't hold back all that goes with it

grief and sorrow
passion and anger
don't tease me with first love
ripping out the chapter on their betrayal

sure, tell me about the living
right after you name the dead
how hope left you
screaming and bleeding
unable to discern nightmares from dreaming

how like a feather it floated away
you lost years chasing after it
reveal how it tickled your feet
when you finally caught up with it

   I'm not really ready for hope
but if you must endorse it
make it so personal it's innately universal

like children in Gaza
making game pieces from the rubble
as the world watches them play
churches sponsor their burial

children in Flint
learning to repurpose fountains
that still can't be used to drink the water

queer kids telling families this is who I am
this the name I call myself now

mothers baking bread for tomorrow
when today's violence is unfathomable
daughters holding their mother's hands
through the unimaginable

grandmothers sitting vigil at the bedside of creation
lighting candles
turning mountains into sleeping bags
oceans into hospitals

artists shaping guns into gardens
bullets into seeds
where magical things grow
like abundance and enough
joy of every fruit and flavor

   I'm not really ready for hope
but if you insist I have it
detach it from your religion
pull god from it all together

make room for an out of town guest
with no date of arrival or departure
make space for the fearful
to loudly whisper why
they are so frightened

pour water on the deniers
and gas-lighters
paint me a picture

use all your pain
every color
make it as vividly abstract as possible
whatever you do
refuse to make it practical
make it so absurd
it's the only way believable

   I'm not really ready for hope
   I'm not ready to go without it either

Small Print

I got my first pair of glasses
in kindergarten
a violet shade of red
after riding my bike
into a phone pole
I didn't see
right in front of me

   late for school
the day I picked them up
I loved them
my classmates laughed
four eyes!
another reason to hide

   40 years later
my vision is changing again
I have to take my glasses off to read
especially small print
it's disorienting
and liberating all at once

navigating the world in new ways
a shifting perspective
of who I am
who god is
both our images
more clear and crisp
revealing oneness and beloved-ness
healing the me that was hidden

Requirements

some requirements are clearly stated
like the sign pasted on the party store door
no shirt, no shoes, no service

the one they added for my young friends and I
only two students at a time

like being at least 48 inches tall to ride
the demon drop at cedar point
like completing five minutes
of treading water in the deep end
and two laps of front crawl to use
                        the diving board

other requirements are more subtle
like bringing your own pencil to take the SAT
your own plate to the potluck
   a mayo-based salad as your dish to pass
wearing a slip under your dress
with itchy tights to church
when all you really want to wear
are basketball shorts and a baseball jersey

I asked my grandmother once
why girls are expected to wear dresses on Sunday

you know, she answered
when I was young
we were also required to wear frilly hats

that's when I really started wondering
what does god require of me
it's got to be more than dresses and frilly hats

I was wearing a baseball hat
when I walked past the entrance
to a pride event
I wasn't out yet
so I never intended to go in
I just wanted to see it
imagine it
what it would be like
to live life free of others' requirements

then I saw this guy with a sign
homosexuals must repent

another read
receive the gospel or burn in hell

and well I just kept walking
wondering what god really requires of me

I didn't know then
there was a scripture with an answer
Micah wasn't on my playlist
or Sunday school memorization chart

the first time I heard these words I cried
what is required of you but to do justice
love kindness, walk humbly with god?

nothing about dresses, slips
itchy tights or being straight
just justice, kindness, humility

I've come to understand more about
doing justice and loving kindness
yet tripped repeatedly
over walking humbly

you see, I thought humility
meant meek and mild
as a child I learned to hide
move without making a sound
blend in with the crowd
dim my light that others not feel outshined
apologize for my very existence

the mother who birthed me used to say
I've never met anyone as pitiful as you

right on cue I'd say
I'm sorry

the mother who gave life to me says,
stop saying you're sorry
why do you apologize for everything

because I'd been taught
that's what walking humbly meant
holding your breath
living lightly so not to leave a footprint

miraculously now I know that's not it

walking humbly
means living intently
paying attention to signs
clear ones, subtle ones
hate filled and hope filled ones
noticing the little ones

like be patient with your server
   we are short staff today
like wear a mask
and stay home if you're feeling sick
   we have high risk people here today

like black lives matter
   act that way
like climate change is real
   live that way
like immigrants are humans too
   behave that way
like christian nationalism is rising
   don't turn the other way
like reproductive rights are also rights
   vote that way
like assault weapons are not sacraments
   don't worship them that way
like queer youth are beloved
   raise your voice and say all the gay
like god is love
   love that way

what's god requiring today
   not shoes
   not shirts
   not dresses
   not slips or frilly hats

a willingness to read the signs
brave the first step in a new direction

Invitation

Hymns are to be sung. Poems to be experienced. Stories to be shared. In addition to this innovative hymnal, Rebecca Wilson is also creating opportunities and resources to accompany individuals and communities composing their own curious faith.

For faith-based audiences, those navigating the trauma faith has inflicted, and for inquiring minds wondering how one expression of faith has risen to such a place of political and social power, Rebecca is an authentic voice and soulful presence, uniquely gifted at bringing people together, speaking gently to harsh realities, and stirring transformation. She speaks hope and breathes healing.

Poetry shows, keynote speaking, sermons, workshops, studies, one-on-one conversations, creative consultations and more, Rebecca is available and excited to partner with you. Visit 10CAMELS.com to dive deeper into the words she is so passionately and prophetically turning into water.

Sample her work at **Wednesdays at the Well** on Substack, where she pours out weekly reflections on the things that cause and quench our thirst.

www.ingramcontent.com/pod-product-compliance
Lightning Source LLC
LaVergne TN
LVHW012105070526
838202LV00056B/5624